REPLANT 101

REPLANT
101

Mark Hallock

ACOMA PRESS

CONTENTS

ACKNOWLEDGMENTS

I want to thank my wonderful wife, Jenna, and my children Zoe and Eli. Thank you for your constant encouragement in my life and ministry. Thanks to Evan Skelton who sacrificed many hours to help make this book what it is. I am so grateful. Finally, thank you to my Calvary Family of Churches' brothers and sisters. I praise God for you.

Soli Deo Gloria.

INTRODUCTION

God is moving.

He is moving in all sorts of unexpected and miraculous ways. He is doing things in and through his Church that are not simply improbable but are impossible. Impossible from a human perspective, that is.

One of the most unexpected and miraculous ways God is moving is through the revitalization and replanting of declining and dying churches throughout North America and beyond. He is bringing life to churches that most people have given up on. Churches that are an afterthought in their communities. Churches that appear headed toward imminent closure once and for all.

God is moving in power to breathe new life and hope to congregations like these in cities and communities just like yours. The book you hold in your hands is designed to introduce you to this movement of God most commonly identified as replanting. More than that, to help you see the role you can play in this movement!

WHO THIS BOOK IS WRITTEN FOR

Replant 101 is written as a companion to a larger volume on the same topic called, *Replant Roadmap*. *Replant Roadmap* is a more thorough resource written to equip the pastors and leaders of a church desiring to replant dying congregations. *Replant 101* serves a different purpose and has a different audience in mind. There are two primary audiences this book is targeting:

#1. Members of churches that are helping to replant a dying congregation. The primary audience I have in mind for this book are the members of a healthy congregation that is seeking to come alongside and replant a dying congregation. This book serves as a basic overview to help educate, guide,

and equip these members to play a vital role in the replanting work their congregation is doing. While *Replant Roadmap* will help equip the leaders of this congregation with the nuts and bolts needed to effectively replant a dying church, *Replant 101* is geared to help equip the members of the replanting congregation come alongside their church leaders in this effort.

#2. Those who simply desire to learn more about replanting. I know there are many who desire to learn more about helping revitalize dying churches through replanting. I hope this book can help serve as a basic introduction of what replanting is, why the need for replanting dying churches is so great, and how they might get involved in some way.

READ *REPLANT 101* ALONE OR IN A GROUP

You may want to work through *Replant 101* on your own, however, it is written to easily allow small groups to work through it together, discussing what they are learning, chapter by chapter. You will notice I have provided discussion questions at the end of each chapter to assist you in this. You may want to have your pastor, or another church leader, lead your Sunday School class or small group through the reading and study of this book. Working through this material together could be of great benefit and always makes learning more enjoyable!

HERE WE GO!

Are you ready for this? I pray the Lord will challenge, encourage, and equip you through this book. I hope it will be a source of joy for you and your walk with the Lord as well. May our great God be pleased, and may Jesus be made famous as together we seek to help dying churches come alive and thrive once again!

Chapter 1

WHAT IS CHURCH REPLANTING?

"Does our church have to die? Can't something be done?"

- Gladys, church member for 47 years

In a day and age when what is valued most in many church circles is big numbers, cool buildings, and over the top programs, it can be incredibly discouraging to be part of a church that has none of these things. A church that from the world's perspective is less than impressive. Adding to that the reality that many of these churches are struggling to simply survive. If you've never been part of a church like this, it may be hard for you to imagine just how tiring and hopeless things can seem at times.

Will things ever get turned around for our church? Do we need to just close the doors for good? Is there any hope? What can we do? Is God done with us?

These are the types of difficult questions men and women, pastors and lay leaders, are wrestling with every day in the thousands of declining and dying churches in North America and beyond. These churches need serious help. They need help from Jesus-loving, Kingdom-minded, mission-focused Christians, congregations, and pastors that share this burden to see forgotten, tired, declining churches reclaimed for the glory of God.

When you look at recent statistics on the health of the church, and Christianity in general, in North America, things don't look so great. Chew on these stats for a few moments:

- According to the Hartford Institute of Religion Research, more than 40 percent of Americans "say" they go to church weekly. As it turns out, however, less than 20 percent are actually in church. In other words, more than 80 percent of Americans are finding other things to do on weekends.[1]

- Each year, nearly 3 million more previous churchgoers enter the ranks of the religiously unaffiliated.[2]

- Barna Group researcher, David Kinnaman, estimates 60 to 80 percent of those raised in the church today in our country will no longer be active in their faith or consider themselves church members by the time they are in their mid-20s.[3]

- Thom Rainer speculates that between 8,000 to 10,000 churches are currently closing their doors every year in North America.[4]

Let me give you a snap shot of the state of churches within one major denomination, the Southern Baptist Convention, which is the largest protestant denomination in North America:

- North American Mission Board research has determined that in recent years, the Southern Baptist Convention has been losing around 900 churches every year.[5]

- Seventy-seven percent of the cities these 900 churches are in have more than 100,000 residents and 90 percent of those churches are in growing communities -- striking down the presumption that declining churches are only in rural or declining areas.[6]

- On average, 17 Southern Baptist churches shut their doors for good every Sunday, leaving underserved and unreached neighborhoods in cities across North America.[7]

- 10-15% of churches in the SBC are healthy and multiplying, 70-75% are plateaued or declining, and 10-15% are at or near risk.[8]

These statistics, among others, are very sobering. What we see is that not only are we in need of new, healthy churches in North America, but we are in desperate need of replanting declining and dying churches. So, what exactly are we talking about when we talk about church replanting?

CHURCH REVITALIZATION VS. CHURCH REPLANTING: WHAT'S THE DIFFERENCE?

Church revitalization and church replanting are two terms you may have heard at some point and are familiar with on a basic level. But how are they distinct? What's the difference between the two? Let's start by considering church revitalization—many of us could take an educated guess on what church revitalization is all about. Hopefully we know it's more than just changing the carpet in a sanctuary or adding some new worship songs! The reality is revitalization is needed in almost every church in our country today.

In church revitalization, the hope and intent is to help a plateaued or declining church get healthy again so that it can become a unified, vibrant, disciple-making congregation on mission to reach their surrounding community with the Gospel. Revitalization is a work only God can do through the power of the Holy Spirit as he works in the heart of a church and its members. Typically, in a revitalization context a church knows they need help, but they may be unaware of just how much help they need. This type of church still has some fight left in them. They have a functional building and enough money and people that they are able to hold out several more years without hitting the panic button. While money, people, and a building can all be great blessings to a church in need of revitalization, these can also help to create a false sense of security that prevents a church from making the necessary changes to become healthy and growing again. In contrast to replanting, the congregation we are describing has no intention of becoming a new or different church; however, it does desire to hire a pastor who will help lead them back to health and vitality.

There are differing mentalities among the congregants within a declining church like this. There are probably some who are saying, "We've really got to do something now! We've got to make some major changes or we're going to die." There may be others who are saying, "Meh, things aren't great, but we're doing okay." Most likely there is probably a third group of folks who are saying, "We're just fine. We don't need to change anything. Are you kidding me? Things are great!" These are typically three of the different types of mindset among the church members of this struggling church. As you can imagine, a church revitalization brings with it great challenges, but also potential opportunities for great Kingdom work.

WHAT IS CHURCH REPLANTING?

Contrary to what you may have heard, church replanting is not the same thing as church revitalization. There are important distinctions. Think of it this way: Church replanting is a specific strategy or approach *to* church revitalization. Broadly speaking, if church revitalization is concerned with helping plateaued or declining churches experience new life and vitality, church replanting is one of the most biblical, God-honoring, and effective strategies for actually making it happen. For the purposes of this book, we will define church replanting as the process by which an existing church is re-launched as a new church, with new leadership (a new replanting pastor), new name, new identity, new governance, new ministry approach and overall new philosophy of ministry.

Church replanting is a very unique ministry. In church replanting, the focus is on congregations that are not simply declining but dying. And they know it. These are congregations that have reached a point where they realize they are not only sick and unhealthy, but they are nearing their death. Churches are first identified as needing to be replanted when they humbly and honestly acknowledge that they are at risk of closing their doors once and for all within two to five years if major changes are not made. These congregations do not simply have a metaphorical cold that needs a little help to get healthy again, but rather they have some form of cancer with major surgery and treatment needed to survive. As a result, these congregations have come to a point of humble surrender. They are no longer concerned with fighting battles over such things as the color of the carpet, whether we sing hymns or praise songs, or whether the pastor preaches in a suit or jeans. They have come to a point of humble surrender, saying, "Lord, whatever you want to do with our church, we are all in. This is your Church, not ours. We want to do whatever it takes to not simply survive, but thrive for the sake of the Gospel, for the sake of this community."

Pastor and church replanting strategist, Jeff Declue, gives a helpful analogy of what replanting is like. Imagine that you were given a beautiful plant. Everyone that came to your house complimented you on its size, health, vibrancy, the breath taking fragrance. Now one day you noticed the plant was changing. Its leaves were turning pale yellow and the plant looked slightly withered. You didn't forget to water it. Maybe someone else watered it too much. Maybe it isn't getting enough light. You love this plant and you will do whatever it takes to save it. If you don't act now it is going to die. Quickly you get the plant into a new pot where you can get back to the basics. You get food with some quality nutrients. You now can make sure it is getting ample sunshine and water. Deep green color starts to return to the leaves and its strength starts to return. It takes time, but it is coming back to life. Now replace the flower in a pot with a church in a community. This is a picture of church "replanting."

Revitalization vs. Replanting:
What is the difference?

Revitalization: A deliberate, dedicated and protracted effort to reverse the decline or death of an existing church.

- The **least** invasive approach as few major changes are made up front.

- Utilizes **existing** structures, leadership and congregants.

- May be led by an existing or **new pastor.**
  Note: Revitalization is less likely to occur successfully with a long tenured existing pastor; more likely, a new pastor will be the best way to move forward.

- Requires a **great deal of time**—the pace of change is very slow.

- **High risk** as the church may reject the leadership efforts of the pastor and leaders and ask them to leave or remove them through elevated conflict or forced termination.

- Is less likely to lead to lasting change and more likely to be a **continuation** of the same.

- Is the **least** effective approach for churches facing imminent closure.

Replant: A decision to close an existing church and re-launch as a new church, with new leadership (a new replanting pastor), new name, new identity, new governance, new ministry approach and overall new philosophy of ministry. In some cases, it is not necessary to adopt a new name but simply adjust it. In some instances where a denominational label is a hindrance to reaching the community or where the name is unnecessarily long or confusing a name change may be appropriate.

- Builds on the **history/legacy** of the previous church.
- Requires **new** leadership (a new replanting pastor).
- New decision-making structure and new decision makers who handle the **daily decisions** (outside transition team).
- New **by-laws** are created and put into practice.
- Offers a break with the past (end date) and a **fresh start** for the future (launch date).
- New **name and identity** can create excitement, momentum, enthusiasm and interest in the community.

As Christians, we need to lock arms and fight to stop the trend of dying churches in our communities. The task of church replanting then is to come alongside these dying congregations and lovingly and joyfully shepherd them back to health, mission, and multiplication. Al Mohler, President of The Southern Baptist Theological Seminary in Louisville, Kentucky writes:

> One of our central tasks in the present generation is to be bold in our vision of replanting churches — helping existing churches to find new vision, new strategic focus, new passion for the gospel, new hunger for the preaching of the Word, new love for their communities, and new excitement about seeing people come to faith in Jesus. Replanting churches requires both courage and leadership skills. A passion for replanting a church must be matched by skills in ministry and a heart for helping a church to regain a vision.[9]

Indeed, the need for church replanting is great, as is the opportunity and potential. Sadly, many churches will close their doors for the final time this next Sunday. As I mentioned earlier, in the Southern Baptist Convention alone, 17 churches will close their doors for the final time this next Sunday. And the next week, another 17 will close. And another 17 the next week. This should break our hearts! Many of these are churches made up of sweet saints who love Jesus, love the Bible and love people, but have perhaps lost vision and hope for what God can do in and through them. They are sheep that need a pastor-shepherd who can know them, feed them, and lead them with passion, joy, and hope into the future. So where do we go from here?

A REPLANTING PATHWAY

Once a church comes to the place of humble surrender and desires to be replanted for the sake of the Gospel and the glory of God, what's next? Practically, what are next steps at this point to begin the replanting process? How does a healthy church and its leaders come alongside and help guide a dying congregation from where they are now to a place of renewed hope and vibrancy through a replanting strategy? Let me offer a brief overview of a replanting pathway that has proven to be effective time and time again with dying churches. This is a pathway that is biblical, pastoral, missional, respectful of history, loving of people, Gospel-driven, and I believe, God-honoring. This is a pathway that is doable and reproducible. It is a pathway that can give thousands of churches hope that indeed God is not done with them.

Here's the replanting pathway I would like to propose in a nutshell. Notice there are three primary components to this pathway—When the dying congregation joyfully chooses to be replanted, they agree to:

1.   **Surrender all day-to-day decision making to an outside transition team, ideally from a sending church.**

2.   **Engage strategic outside ministry partners.**

3.   **Call a trained replanting pastor.**

What does this pathway look like practically? First, as noted above, the church needing to be replanted has already said, "We surrender. We recognize this is the Lord's church and to move forward in a healthy way, there needs to be fresh leadership. We joyfully submit to an outside transition team that can guide us into the future." This transition team could be a group of pastors, elders, deacons or other lay leaders from a particular Sending Church that will oversee and lead this replanting process. The team could be a group made up of pastors and leaders from different churches in the community. It could be a group of denominational leaders. It might be a combination of all the above. Whoever these individuals are that make up the transition team, the dying church has agreed to give up day-to-day decision making and oversight to this outside group of leaders. They have gladly surrendered to this group to help guide them and lead them into the future.

Secondly, the congregation, along with their outside transition team, begins to engage outside ministry partners and churches, inviting them to be part of this new, exciting replanting vision. The reality is that no declining church can get healthy on its own. Declining churches need healthy churches to come alongside them, to encourage them, help share resources with them, and joyfully serve as partners in this new work. Radical cooperation is needed. This is the beauty of the body of Christ in action and makes much of Jesus and the Gospel!

Thirdly, the congregation recognizes they need a pastor who is trained in, equipped for, and has a heart for replanting. Because replanting is a unique ministry, it takes unique leadership, including a unique type of pastor. This church needs a pastor who is a visionary shepherd. This is a pastor who is burdened to reach the lost in the community and who is willing to do whatever it takes to lead this dying church to engage the surrounding community with the love of Christ. At the same time, this congregation needs a pastor who truly loves shepherding people, both young and old, who respects and honors the history of the congregation and understands the unique dynamics of replanting ministry. Where does this church find such a pastor? In most cases, this replanting pastor will be identified and appointed by the transition team (mentioned above) that is helping to oversee the entire replanting process for this congregation. Working with the declining congregation and potentially denominational leaders, the transition team will seek to find a replanter who they believe is a good fit for leading this particular congregation back to health and life.

Can you imagine what would happen if we began to see large numbers of declining churches begin to pursue this kind of replanting pathway? I can tell you from experience, more and more churches are choosing to trust the Lord and take a leap of faith in this very direction. Many once dying churches are now becoming healthy again, engaging their communities and reaching the lost with the power of Christ in new and exciting ways. Children's Sunday School classrooms that had been empty for years are now filled with laughter and singing from little ones each and every Sunday morning. Baptism tanks that had been dry and unused for years are now being filled regularly as lost men and women experience new life in Jesus. Neighborhoods that for years had not even taken notice or cared that a church had been there is now taking notice, being impacted in countless ways through new outreach ministries making a real difference in the community. It's happening! The Lord is doing this kind of replanting work all over our country and world for his glory and the joy of his Church.

WE'RE NOT TALKING ONE REPLANT HERE... WE'RE TALKING A MOVEMENT

As excited as I get at the thought of even one dying church being replanted for the sake of the Gospel, the truth is, in order to reach the masses of people in our world that don't know Christ, *one replant is not enough*. Two are not enough. Ten are not enough. Even a hundred new church replants are not enough! Our vision as the church in North America must be to see hundreds and even thousands of churches replanted for the glory of God. What we need is a *replanting movement*. A cyclical movement of churches replanting churches that replant churches.

Now, what exactly do I mean by a movement? What is a replanting movement? On the most basic level, movements are about mobilizing people behind a shared purpose. Movements happen in our world all the time. Movements happen in the world of business, or technology, or food, or entertainment, or even in the church. When you look at the spread of the Gospel through the early church in the book of Acts, what you see is a movement…a Gospel movement infused by the Holy Spirit that changed the world, one life, one church, one community, at a time.

I don't know about you, but I get excited dreaming about a new kind of movement in the church today. A church replanting movement. A movement where God does what only he can do through his people. A movement where God uses ordinary, faithful pastors, church leaders, and lay people to bring declining and dying churches back to life. A movement that mobilizes God's people behind the shared purpose of replanting dying churches for the glory of God. A movement where churches that seem to have no hope and no pulse come back to life by the Spirit of God in such a way that they not only survive but thrive to the point of replanting other dying congregations.

Yes, we need to plant new churches. We need to plant many new churches in order to take the Gospel to areas where people are far from Christ. But at the same time, if we as the Church of Jesus Christ are going to truly push back the darkness and go from a posture of defense to a posture of offense in our mission to take the light of Christ into a dark world, we must be as intentional and purposeful in our church replanting efforts as we are in our church planting efforts. It is not an either/or, but rather, a both/and. Now is the time. Now is the time for a church replanting movement. Are you in?

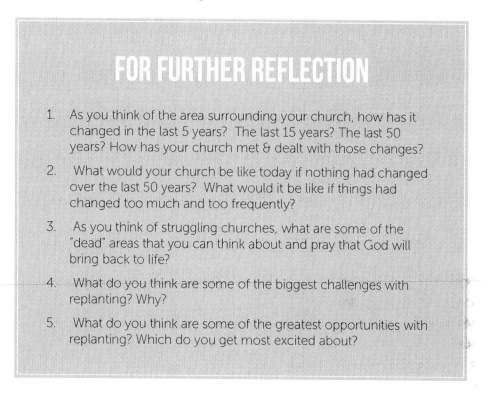

FOR FURTHER REFLECTION

1. As you think of the area surrounding your church, how has it changed in the last 5 years? The last 15 years? The last 50 years? How has your church met & dealt with those changes?

2. What would your church be like today if nothing had changed over the last 50 years? What would it be like if things had changed too much and too frequently?

3. As you think of struggling churches, what are some of the "dead" areas that you can think about and pray that God will bring back to life?

4. What do you think are some of the biggest challenges with replanting? Why?

5. What do you think are some of the greatest opportunities with replanting? Which do you get most excited about?

Chapter 2

WHY IS REPLANTING SO IMPORTANT?

I'm just not convinced that replanting churches is a good way to go. I've seen so many churches that 'say' they want to get healthy, but when it comes down to it, they're not willing to do what it really takes to get there. I mean, come on Mark, do you really believe replanting churches is a wise use of time, money, and other resources? Wouldn't it be more effective to just let these dying churches die?

This was a conversation I had recently over coffee with a pastor friend of mine. I wish I could say this conversation was the only one of its kind, but I hear these concerns regularly from pastors and church leaders all over the country. Is my friend, right? Is this replanting thing a waste of time? Is it worth all of the sacrificial energy and resources and prayer we put into it? Are we just being unwise here? Is it better to just let these churches die? Are there better places to put our funds and efforts? These are good questions that deserve thoughtful answers. Let me share some of my thoughts on this by offering seven reasons why I believe my friend (whom I love dearly) is wrong. These are seven reasons why I believe it is absolutely critical that churches, just like yours, begin to actively and intentionally pursue the replanting and revitalization of dying churches in our communities.

REASON #1: GOD'S PEOPLE IN DYING CHURCHES NEED ENCOURAGEMENT, NOURISHMENT AND FRESH VISION

First of all, God's people in dying churches need **encouragement**. Typically, when you step inside a dying church, you will quickly see folks who are *tired*. They're exhausted. They've probably lost passion and zeal. It's not that they desire to be dispassionate about the Lord, the church, and the lost. It's just that they've been going so hard for so long that they're simply worn out. It's been a difficult season for that church, and likely the season has been a long one. This church needs encouragement - lots of loving encouragement.

Secondly, God's people in dying churches need nourishment. The Lord's sheep need nourishment. Sheep rely on receiving healthy food from a good shepherd, a pastor who faithfully preaches and teaches the Word of God. John 21:15 says, "When they had finished eating, Jesus said to Simon Peter, 'Simon, son of John, do you truly love me more than these?' 'Yes Lord,' he said, 'You know that I love you.' Jesus said, 'Feed my lambs.'" It's the responsibility of a replanting pastor to feed the flock of God good food for the renewing of their hearts and minds that they might move out on mission in their community with joy and strength in the Lord. This is why raising up and training faithful replanting pastors is so critical to seeing churches replanted in a healthy, biblical way. Jeremiah 3:15 reads, "The Lord declares, I will give you shepherds after my own heart who will lead you with knowledge and understanding." Dying congregations need replanting pastors who can shepherd them well, nourishing them with the food of God's Word, while leading them with knowledge and understanding.

Thirdly, God's people in dying churches need fresh vision. Many times these churches have lost vision. As a result, they have lost hope and passion for what the Lord can do in and through their congregation. They need fresh vision and new hope. They need to be loved and led in such a way that they begin to believe the truth that God isn't done with their church. More than that, they need to believe that God is just getting started with what he wants to do in and through them for his purposes!

REASON #2: THE LOST IN OUR COMMUNITIES NEED TO SEE CONGREGATIONS ALIVE AND ON MISSION

Sadly, all too often declining churches have become "non-factors" in their communities. Where perhaps at one time this church was a central hub serving various needs in the community, they have become nothing more than an eyesore to those in the neighborhood. Sadly, I have visited with non-believers in different cities who would just as soon see dying churches in their neighborhoods disappear and become restaurants or apartment complexes than for them to remain as they are -- non-factors in the neighborhood. This must never be. How desperately neighborhoods all across our country need these declining churches to be replanted and become lighthouses for Jesus once again. Replanted churches serve as a source of true hope and encouragement, love and healing for people in their communities. The lost and the broken in these communities need the church, simply because they need Jesus.

REASON #3: WE HAVE A BIBLICAL MANDATE TO MAKE DISCIPLES WHO MAKE DISCIPLES

As his followers, Jesus has given us a clear mission. Our mission is to make disciples who make disciples. It is that simple. This is what we're called to do both as individuals and as congregations. Jesus is speaking to his disciples in Matthew 28:18 – 20, when we read these familiar words:

> And Jesus came and said to them, "All authority in heaven and on earth has been given to me. Go therefore and make disciples of all nations, baptizing them in the name of the Father and of the Son and of the Holy Spirit, teaching them to observe all that I have commanded you. And behold I am with you always, to the end of the age."

Jesus couldn't be clearer. The mission of the church is to make disciples of all nations, baptizing them and teaching them to obey all that he's commanded. He promises to be our strength and to be with us as we seek to follow his commands. We must replant churches so the lost can be saved and discipled in the way of Jesus, that they might then go and disciple others. Simply put, more joyful, passionate disciples of Jesus will be made as we replant dying congregations.

REASON #4: GOD IS HONORED AS WE STEWARD MONEY, BUILDINGS, AND OTHER RESOURCES

One of the great blessings of replanting a congregation is the opportunity to steward God-given resources that have been handed down throughout the history of a declining congregation. This is another reason why we need to become more serious about and passionate about replanting. Matt Schmucker is right when he writes:

> Billions of dollars, donated by faithful Christians over many decades, have been invested in land and buildings. Today, those buildings are too often underutilized or even empty—mere monuments to the past. Church planters often shun these resources and don't think twice about pursuing the potentially life-consuming "mobile church" or "church on wheels" approach to ministry.
>
> Why is this approach so consuming? Ask almost any planter. He'll probably tell you how much effort it takes from his best people in the church to re-set every week, let alone to relocate when a school auditorium or hotel ballroom is lost. So consider moving into an old neighborhood, revitalizing a church, and reclaiming resources that were originally given for gospel purposes.[1]

I think Matt is right on here. The Lord has been honored in the past through faithful Christians who have given generously to church building funds and other physical resources. We're called to be stewards of these generous past gifts as we seek to reach the surrounding community with the love of Christ.

REASON #5: REVITALIZED AND REPLANTED CHURCHES BRING HOPE TO OTHERS

I hope we would all agree that when we look at the New Testament, we see a constant theme of Christian encouragement. We are to encourage one another. We are to spur one another on, to build one another up. This is true not only as individuals, but also as churches. There is nothing more encouraging to a declining congregation than to see other dying congregations be replanted, transformed and coming back to life.

What a joy it is to visit with many dying churches and to share stories of the new life the Lord has brought to other congregations just like them through replanting. To hear the stories and see pictures and meet the people of those churches helps them to see there is hope! That God is not finished with their church either.

REASON #6: OTHER DECLINING CHURCHES NEED FRESH VISION, IDEAS, AND MINISTRY STRATEGIES

Dying churches receive hope when they see other struggling churches come back to life. But they receive more than just hope. There are also all kinds of practical ideas and ministry strategies that are gained in working with and learning from former declining churches. This is yet another great joy in church replanting—it's not just for the sake of one church getting healthy, but churches helping one another to become healthy again.

The vision we must have as leaders in the church when it comes to this conversation of replanting is not to see one or two churches become healthy again, but to see an entire movement of churches replanted for the glory of God. Many churches that were once close to death, coming back to health and life again. This happens as replanted churches radically cooperate with dying congregations that they might share with them fresh vision, ideas and ministry resources of various kinds. We are in this together.

REASON #7: WE DESIRE THE PRAISE AND GLORY OF GOD'S NAME THROUGHOUT THE EARTH

This is the ultimate goal, the ultimate end, in church replanting because it is the ultimate goal, the ultimate end of all creation. The reason that God's glory must be our ultimate goal is because he *alone* is worthy of glory. God desires to be glorified and he has invited us to joyfully pursue the glory of his name in our lives and ministries. This includes the replanting of churches. There's probably no text in the Bible that reveals the passion that God has for his own glory more than what we see in Isaiah 48:9 – 11. This is where we read the Lord speaking,

> For my name's sake I defer my anger, for the sake of my praise I restrain it for you, that I may not cut you off. Behold, I have refined you, but not as silver; I have tried you in the furnace of affliction. For my own sake, for my own sake, I do it, for how should my name be profaned? My glory I will not give to another.

We're reminded in this text that the Lord has allowed many churches to struggle and go through difficult seasons, ultimately for his glory. But here's the reality: God, in his love, grace, and kindness, brings churches back from near death for his glory too. He desires servants, leaders, followers, and congregations who are humble enough to say, "Lord, this is all about you! This is not my church, this is Your church. This is the bride of Christ that Jesus died to save. Lord, be glorified in us. Be glorified in this church. For Your glory alone, Lord!"

Matt Schmucker writes:

> For the sake of God's name being rightly represented in the world, we need to be jealous for the witness of his church. Why? So that God's glory might be spread and magnified. His name is defamed when so-called Christian churches misrepresent him with tolerance of sin, their bad marriage practices, wrong views on sexuality, and a host of heresies from salvation to the authority of Scripture.
>
> I pray against those churches that would defame God's name. I pray they would die or at least be invisible to the neighborhood.
>
> I positively pray for those true churches in my neighborhood that proclaim truth, that rightly gather those who have been born again, and whose ultimate purpose is God's glory. Consider revitalizing for the sake of God's name.[2]

God is about his glory. We must be about his glory as well. Mark Clifton has written extensively on this very topic of replanting churches for the sake of God's fame and God's glory. He writes:

> A dying church robs God of His Glory. The key to revitalization of a church near death is a passion for the Glory of God in all things. This alone must be the beginning and primary motivation for a Legacy replant, even over worthy objectives such as reaching the community, growing the church and meeting needs. The purpose of all creation is the glory of God. He created everything for His own glory.[3]

As Romans 11:36 proclaims, "For of him and through him and to him are all things, to whom be glory forever." Clifton is right— All things are to bring glory to the Lord. This is true in church replanting. We want to see the glory of God spread to the ends of the earth as we see hopeless situations and dying churches redeemed for his fame.

GOD HAS ALWAYS BEEN IN THIS BUSINESS

We want to see churches come back to life. Even ones that some have looked at and said, "It's all over - No hope there." God has always been in the business of bringing dead things back to life (namely his own Son, Jesus). In the same way, he is in the business of bringing dying churches back to life. his desire is the same in our churches today.

FOR FURTHER REFLECTION

1. What are some of the reasons why replanting churches is so important in our day and age? Can you think of some reasons beyond those mentioned in this chapter?

2. How many of us have made new year's resolutions to get healthy? How many of us actually did get healthy? Why or why not? Many churches say they want to get healthy, but they don't want to do the things needed to move in a healthy direction. Why do you think that is?

3. What does it look like to live life alive & on mission? What difference does it make if outsiders/non-believers see this in a church or not?

4. Throughout history, the Gospel has been spread through disciples who are making disciples - who was one person who God used to make a big difference in your spiritual growth? How do you create this kind of disciple reproducing culture in a church?

5. In the cycle of church replanting, the vision is for a church to go from dying to becoming healthy to being able to be a church that replants others. What components are needed for this to become a reality? List and discuss.

Chapter 3

WHAT DOES GOD SAY ABOUT REPLANTING CHURCHES?

God does his best work when things seem hopeless. He always has. This is true when it comes to working in the lives of individuals, and it is also true when it comes to working in the lives of dying churches. God's heart is *for* his church, *including* churches that are dying. When considering the topic of God's heart for replanting, there are four biblical convictions that are critical for us to hold. If these are not believed at the very core, I would question whether you are truly on board with the work of church replanting.

CONVICTION #1: GOD DESIRES TO SEE DYING AND DECLINING CHURCHES COME BACK TO LIFE

I hope you believe this. My guess is if you have read this far, you do indeed believe this. Without a doubt, God desires to see dying and declining churches come back to life. One of the many things I love about God and Scripture is that it is so clear that in our weakness, he is strong. He's always looking for humble servants that he can use for his purposes and to bring glory to himself. We must become less so that he might become more. Here's the thing about the Lord: unlike our fallen world, he uses and loves underdogs! Everywhere in the Scriptures, whether you're talking David and Goliath, or Jesus' disciples, or the Apostle Paul, the Lord always goes after and uses the "wrong" people. He chooses players on his team that you and

I would never choose. He chooses the weak, the foolish, the uncool, and uses them in mighty ways.

This is the heart of God. This is the heart of God for individuals and for churches. God loves underdog churches. He loves it when the world is saying, "That church is dead and done. That church just needs to shut the doors." That's when God says, "You watch. I'm ready to do my best work right here, right now." The Lord is like that, and he's always been that way. Let's praise him for it!

In 2 Corinthians, chapter 12, verses 9-10, the Apostle Paul writes this:

> But he said to me, "My grace is sufficient for you, for my power is made perfect in weakness." Therefore, I will boast all the more gladly of my weaknesses, so that the power of Christ may rest upon me. For the sake of Christ, then, I am content with weaknesses, insults, hardships, persecutions, and calamities. For when I am weak, then I am strong.

This is key to every one of us as believers and leaders in Christ's Church—that when we are weak, we are strong in the Lord. It's true as churches and congregations, as well. When a church recognizes it's weakness and brokenness, it is then in a place of humility where the Lord does his best work. It is in that place that God does the impossible. It is in that place that God makes a church strong again and brings it back to life for his glory.

Years ago, I came across a powerful quote from the great Baptist preacher Charles Spurgeon that I come back to often. Concerning weakness and humility in ministry, Spurgeon writes,

> A primary qualification for serving God with any amount of success, and for doing God's work well and triumphantly, is a sense of our own weakness. When God's warrior marches forth to battle, strong in his own might, when he boasts, "I know that I shall conquer, my own right arm and my conquering sword shall get unto me the victory," defeat is not far distant. God will not go forth with that man who marches in his own strength. He who reckoneth on victory thus has reckoned wrongly, for "it is not by might, nor by power, but by my Spirit, saith the Lord of hosts." They who go forth to fight, boasting of their prowess, shall return with their banners trailed in the dust, and their armour stained with disgrace.[1]

What a great yet convicting image. How often we seek to go forth in battle by our own strength. What foolishness! What pride! Spurgeon goes on,

> Those who serve God must serve Him in His own way, and in His strength, or He will never accept their service. That which man doth, unaided by divine strength, God can never own. The mere fruits of the earth He casteth away; He will only reap that corn, the seed of which was sown from heaven, watered by grace, and ripened by the sun of divine love. God will empty out all that thou hast before He will put His own into thee; He will first clean out thy granaries before He will fill them with the finest of the wheat.[2]

In other words, until we recognize our emptiness and weakness, he can't fill us with the power of his Spirit. And if you're like me, I not only want, but know I need, his power. I need his power more than anything in my life and ministry.

And then listen to Spurgeon's final words of hope and encouragement:

> The river of God is full of water; but not one drop of it flows from earthly springs. God will have no strength used in His battles but the strength which He Himself imparts.
>
> Are you mourning over your own weakness? Take courage, for there must be a consciousness of weakness before the Lord will give thee victory. Your emptiness is but the preparation for your being filled, and your casting down is but the making ready for your lifting up.[3]

Such wise and truth-filled words for each of us. Let me offer two simple but important points of application, the first being personal for each of us. As pastors and church leaders, we must understand and embrace this truth: Until we empty ourselves, humbling ourselves before the Lord, he will not do what he wants to do in us and through us. The Lord doesn't need us—he doesn't need anything. But, it is his delight to use us and invite us into his work of ministry and mission in the world.

A second application is for dying and declining churches. Until a congregation humbles itself, and recognizes its need, this church should not expect the Lord to pour out his Spirit and bring dead bones back to life. He is looking for a humble and dependent people who seek to make a big deal about him as they joyfully submit to his Word and his will.

Remember, both in our personal lives and in our churches, God loves to give strength to the needy. To those who are desperate for him. Will we be those kinds of people? Those kinds of churches?

In John 7:37 – 39, Jesus says this:

> On the last day of the feast, the great day, Jesus stood up and cried out, "If anyone thirsts, let him come to me and drink. Whoever believes in me, as the Scripture has said, 'Out of his heart will flow rivers of living water.'" Now this he said about the Spirit, whom those who believed in him were to receive, for as yet the Spirit had not been given, because Jesus was not yet glorified.

Jesus is pointing to the indwelling power of the Holy Spirit we need as individuals, leaders, and churches. I often pray that the church I serve will be filled with the Holy Spirit of God and that many would be saved by the Spirit. That marriages would be restored. That children, at a young age, would come to a saving faith in Christ. This is what I desire to see in our church, and the Spirit of God desires to see this far more than I do. He always has. But it begins with us, as his people, humbling ourselves in faith, asking and believing that the Lord can do these things according to his perfect will. It begins with each of us on our knees, praying with David in Psalm 51:10–12: "Create in me a clean heart, O God, and renew a right spirit within me. Cast me not away from your presence and take not your Holy Spirit from me. Restore to me the joy of your salvation and uphold me with a willing spirit."

May this prayer be the cry of our hearts as individuals and as churches. The hard truth is this: Any church that cannot pray the prayer, "Oh God create in us a clean heart, renew us, revive us, humble us" is too prideful, too proud, too hard-hearted. If they can't pray that prayer, that church should not expect God to do miraculous things and bring that church back to life. Our posture must always be one of humility before the Lord.

CONVICTION #2: GOD HAS THE POWER TO BRING DYING AND DECLINING CHURCHES BACK TO LIFE

I hope you believe this. When it comes to replanting dying churches, God isn't sitting there wringing his hands and saying, "Oh boy, I sure wish that kind of thing could happen, but I really don't have the power to do anything about it." No, the Lord is the all-powerful, sovereign King of the universe. He not only has the desire but also the power to bring anything that is dead back to life, including a local church.

Ezekiel 37 is a great picture of the Lord bringing something dead back to life. At this point, both Jerusalem and the temple have been destroyed. Judgment has come. But God reveals himself in this passage as a God of revitalization; as a God of resurrection.

In Ezekiel 37:1-6 we read this,

> The hand of the LORD was upon me, and he brought me out in the Spirit of the LORD and set me down in the middle of the valley; it was full of bones. And he led me around among them, and behold, there were very many on the surface of the valley, and behold, they were very dry. And he said to me, "Son of man, can these bones live?" And I answered, "O Lord GOD, you know." Then he said to me, "Prophesy over these bones, and say to them, O dry bones, hear the word of the LORD. Thus says the Lord GOD to these bones: Behold, I will cause breath to enter you, and you shall live. And I will lay sinews upon you, and will cause flesh to come upon you, and cover you with skin, and put breath in you, and you shall live, and you shall know that I am the LORD."

Only our God can do something as powerful and miraculous as bringing dead, dry bones back to life. He does this very thing with us as individuals and he does it with churches. There are two things that I want to point out from this passage, two essential ingredients for revitalization in the church that I think we see in this passage. The first one is this:

Ingredient#1: The faithful preaching of God's Word is essential to God-honoring replanting and true church revitalization.

In his excellent book *Can These Dry Bones Live?*, Bill Henard writes,

> The first requirement necessitates the preaching of God's Word. God tells Ezekiel, "Prophesy concerning those bones" (37:4). As Ezekiel obeys, the Scripture unveils this magnificent vision of bones taking on tendons and flesh. Note carefully that the bones described are dry bones. These soldiers who died in battle were not afforded the privilege of a proper burial. They experienced the great disgrace of open decay. Yet God intervenes, and Ezekiel speaks to the bones.[4]

What an image as we think about church replanting and revitalization. The preaching of God's Word has the power to bring dry bones, souls, and churches back to life. It is living and active as we preach, counsel with and share the Word with folks over coffee and meals. The Word of God brings dry, dead bones back to life.

Ingredient #2: The presence and power of the Holy Spirit.

The second ingredient for revitalization that we see here in this passage is the presence and power of God's Spirit. Again, Henard writes,

> In order for the church to be revived, (to be revitalized, to experience new life, new health, new growth) it will demand a mighty work of God's Spirit. Following a particular methodology or program does not guarantee success. One might greatly desire for the church to revitalize and grow, but genuine church growth calls for more than personal passion. It requires the Spirit of God.[5]

That is the truth. We can read all the books we want. We can come up with the most dynamic, exciting, fresh, and compelling strategies the world of church revitalization and church replanting has ever seen, but without the Spirit of God moving, dead bones don't come back to life. They just don't. Church revitalization and replanting begins with laying the foundation of God's Word as it is preached and the congregation empowered by a profound movement of God's Spirit.

CONVICTION #3: TRUE REVITALIZATION, REQUIRES A RETURN TO A CONGREGATION'S FIRST LOVE—JESUS.

Dry bones won't come back to life and churches won't be revitalized unless a church returns to its first love, which is Jesus Christ. In Revelation 2:1-5, we read words that perhaps many of us in the church are familiar with. In this passage, the Lord is speaking to the church at Ephesus:

> To the angel of the church in Ephesus write: "The words of him who holds the seven stars in his right hand, who walks among the seven golden lampstands. 'I know your works, your toil and your patient endurance, and how you cannot bear with those who are evil, but have tested those who call themselves apostles and are not, and found them to be false. I know you are

enduring patiently and bearing up for my name's sake, and you have not grown weary.'"

This is a great church! This is a church that is steady and faithful. This is a church that has endured much, all the while remaining steadfast in the Lord. This is a congregation that is rock solid when it comes to understanding sound doctrine. This is a church that loves the Bible. There is much to be commended in this church. But notice what Jesus says next, in verses 4 and 5:

> But I have this against you, that you have abandoned the love you had at first. Remember therefore from where you have fallen; repent, and do the works you did at first. If not, I will come to you and remove your lampstand from its place, unless you repent.

The picture here is of a church that has its doctrine right, its missions giving is probably greater than any other in its local church association, it's doing all kinds of things right, and yet when Jesus looks at the heart of this church, he sees a people that are no longer in love with him. They may say they are, but they aren't really. Their passion for Christ has dwindled. There's no zeal for the things of God. The study of God's Word has become simply an academic exercise. The Word is no longer setting the heart of this church on fire for evangelism and missions. Its head perhaps, but not its heart. And so the Lord says, "If you don't return to your first love, if you don't do those things you did at first when you had a simple, childlike faith in me and love for me, unless you repent and turn back to me, I'm going to take your lampstand away."

Mark Clifton says that in this passage, the Lord makes it clear that the pathway to new life for a dying church is repentance and remembering. Those are two key words for any church that wants to be revitalized— repent and remember. But Clifton clarifies what this type of remembering means exactly:

> ...not the self-serving nostalgia of remembering the past for the sake of our own edification through control and a desire to return to a "better time", but remembering the legacy of missions and ministry that first birthed this dying church and a brokenness to see that return once again. This kind of remembering can only happen if repentance comes first. This kind of

remembering can only happen when the Glory of God becomes primary rather than the glory of the past.[6]

There's one main reason why a church dies— because it loses it's first love. It is when we lose our first love that we begin to lose everything. We lose our love for the truth. We lose our love for the lost. We lose everything. When we lose our love for the Lord and the things of the Lord, we increase our love for self and our own "kingdom" rather than God's. And so we must beg God in all humility, "Oh Lord, change our hearts. Turn our hearts back toward you, that you would be the love and passion of our lives. Lord, may you be our greatest treasure in this life and forevermore!"

CONVICTION #4: GOD BRINGS ABOUT REVITALIZATION THROUGH THREE TYPES OF RENEWAL

When a church comes to the point of genuine humility, returning to Jesus and the Gospel as its first love, then and only then does God begin to bring about true renewal and revitalization. He does this through three types of renewal.[7]

Renewal #1: Personal Renewal

When a dying congregation's leaders experience personal renewal, true congregational renewal begins. This starts with the heart of the leaders. Personal renewal means that leaders in the church recognize the need for more of the Holy Spirit. These leaders begin to grow in humility, love for people, and love for the lost. As leaders we cannot take people where we've never been. We cannot give what we do not have. This is why congregational renewal begins with personal renewal. And this is why our love for the Lord and his Word must be primary.

Renewal #2: Relational Renewal

In a church where leaders begin to experience personal renewal, relational renewal should naturally begin to follow. Relational renewal means that leaders are not only right with God, but now they are getting right with others. The leaders in a congregation are doing all they can to pursue peace, unity, and harmony with others in the congregation. Reconciliation marked by genuine kindness and love for other brothers and sisters in Christ should be a top priority. Rick Warren says this,

> When you have relational renewal in your church, the gossip goes down and the joy goes up. How do you know when a church has been through relational renewal? People hang around longer after the service. They want to spend time together. If people don't want to hang around after your services, you have a performance, not a church. The church is more than content; it's a community.[8]

Renewal #3: Missional Renewal

As leaders grow in their love for God and he begins to renew their hearts, it spreads out to others and results in relational renewal. This then begins to lead a congregation outside the walls of the church on mission. It's inevitable—if the Spirit of God renews us the Spirit of God is going to align our desires with God's desires; namely, living life on mission, seeking to reach those in the community with the good news of the Gospel.

This type of missional renewal is seen not only in the leadership but will spread through the congregation as individuals and families grow in their passion and conviction to make disciples of Jesus. When missional renewal begins to happen, a church begins to both believe they need to reach the lost and are willing to do whatever it takes to do it. It is when a church begins to experience this third type of renewal that God begins to do incredible things in a dying church. This is when replanting gets really fun! Seeing a church get back on mission, focusing no longer on itself and its survival but on the lost and the surrounding community that deeply needs Jesus. This is God's desire for dying churches. This is God's heart for replanting and revitalization.

GOD LOVES HIS CHURCH

God loves his church. He loves his people. He loves to bring dead bones back to life. In this way, his heart is to breathe new life into dying congregations for the salvation of the lost, the joy of his people, and for the spread of his fame throughout the earth. From the world's perspective, there seems to be little hope for dying churches. However, when we see the heart of God in his Word, we have much reason for hope. Hope that God will do what only he can do: breathe new life into the dry, dusty bones of churches all over the world for his glory.

FOR FURTHER REFLECTION

1. Read 2 Corinthians 12:9-10 - why do you think that God often seems to work more in the weak places in our lives, and with the seemingly hopeless situations?

2. Until we recognize our weakness, and our need to rely on God's strength, he can't fill us with his Spirit and his power. How do we help churches to name reality and become more aware of their weakness & lack of power in a way that leads to greater surrender to God?

3. What are the types of renewal that God brings about? How do they interact with each other? Which is most difficult? Why?

Chapter 4

HOW DO I GET INVOLVED IN REPLANTING?

Perhaps you are sitting there and you are sold on this idea of church replanting. You understand the sad reality that congregations in our country are sick and dying and they need radical help. The question is this: How can you, and your church, get involved in the replanting of dying churches? I want to encourage you to consider four specific ways you can get involved in the replanting of dying churches right now. As you consider these four avenues of involvement, perhaps you will need to find a specific replant to partner with if your current congregation isn't already connected to one. If this is the case, you may want to reach out to pastors or denominational leaders who may be aware of new replants being started in your area. You can also find a helpful list of current replants at churchreplanters.com. Simply click on the Replant Map and find a replant near you that you can begin building a relationship with. Let's briefly consider four ways you can get involved.

#1: PRAY FOR PARTICULAR REPLANTS AND THEIR LEADERS

As with other types of ministry, those involved in church replanting need faithful prayer support. I'm reminded of Ephesians 6:18–20, where the Apostle Paul unapologetically asks the Christians in Ephesus to pray for him and his ministry:

> …at all times in the Spirit, with all prayer and supplication. To that end keep alert with all perseverance, making supplication for all the saints, and also for me, that words may be given to me in opening my mouth boldly to proclaim

the mystery of the Gospel, for which I am an ambassador in chains, that I may declare it boldly, as I ought to speak.

Prayer must be a top priority in our church replanting efforts. Let me share twelve specific ways you can intentionally be in prayer for both replanters and their families, as well as newly replanted congregations. It would be worthwhile to ask others to join you in praying for these twelve things on a regular and consistent basis.

12 Prayers for Replants and Replanters

1. Pray for a particular church replant and its leaders, that they will keep their eyes on God, not taking a step apart from his leading.

2. Pray for courage and boldness to go where the Lord leads them.

3. Pray for humility before the Lord and people, prioritizing the raising up of other leaders in the replant.

4. Pray the replant and its leaders will not rely on their own strength, but trust in the Lord's strength.

5. Pray for a deep heart of love and grace in those leading this new replant.

6. Pray for the health of marriages and families in this replanted congregation.

7. Pray the replant and its leaders will walk worthy of the calling God has placed on their lives.

8. Pray for the replanter to preach the Word and the Gospel boldly.

9. Pray for God to destroy idols in the hearts of the leaders and in the hearts of those in the congregation.

10. Pray for God-honoring unity in the congregation.

11. Pray the replant and its leaders will do whatever it takes to reach the lost in their community.

12. Pray for the making of disciples who make disciples in and through the replant.

Consider adding specific prayer requests to this list of twelve on a regular basis. Ask the pastor and leaders of a new replant for specific prayer requests that you can bring before the Lord on their behalf. Be sure to let these leaders know you are praying for them. There is nothing more encouraging than knowing other brothers and sisters are praying on your behalf!

Another way you can help:
Connect a dying church with good counsel

Perhaps there is a particular church you are aware of that is really struggling. They are trying to figure out how to turn things around before they have to close their doors for good. You can be a huge help to this church. How? You can help the leaders of this congregation pursue needed counsel and wisdom from voices outside of their church. The Bible is very clear that wisdom comes when we seek godly counsel from others. This is particularly true when we find ourselves at a major crossroads in our life and it isn't clear which way the Lord wants us to go. Perhaps you know of a church that is at that type of crossroads right now. The book of Proverbs is filled with verses that speak to the importance of seeking godly counsel. Consider these:

- *The way of a fool is right in his own eyes, but a wise man listens to advice.* – Proverbs 12:15

- *Where there is no guidance, a people falls, but in an abundance of counselors there is safety.* – Proverbs 11:14

- *Without counsel plans fail, but with many advisers they succeed.* – Proverbs 15:22

You can come alongside and help a declining church pursue this type of godly counsel at this point in time. Wisdom that comes from godly individuals who are not part of their church. These men and women can offer insight and helpful perspective as those who are not intimately connected to this struggling congregation. They can help a church think through tough questions and issues pertaining to their future in an unbiased, godly, objective manner. So who exactly are these outside counselors you can help a struggling congregation seek counsel from? Where do you find them? Here are three groups to consider pursuing.

Group #1: Denominational & Network Leaders

Contact area denominational and network leaders. These leaders exist for the sole purpose of helping churches to be more effective in gospel ministry. Most of these leaders have been trained on some level to come alongside declining and struggling churches to help bring support, encouragement, counsel, and connections who can also be of assistance in this time. These leaders can also bring helpful resources to help replant or revitalize this church moving forward.

Group #2: Seminaries & Bible Schools

You can reach out to seminaries and Bible schools in your area. Many times, you will find professors at seminaries who have experience pastoring in local church contexts and specialize in helping churches that are dying. It is well worth connecting with one of these schools to see if there is a faculty member that the leaders from a declining church can speak with. Most likely, you will find someone who can offer helpful insight for their situation, as well as connect them to others who can be of help.

Group #3: Local Pastors & Churches

Connect with local pastors and churches in your community. There are many pastors and churches in your community that would love to help this dying church in some way. At a minimum, you will find pastors and individuals in these churches that would love to come alongside and offer godly wisdom and counsel to this congregation.

However, along with counsel, many times there are leaders in churches within your community who would love to see their congregation partner with this congregation, as they seek to become a healthy, vibrant church once again. Unfortunately, while there are always some who feel threatened by other churches in their community, I believe there are many others that care more about the Kingdom of God than just their own church. As Christians, we are all in this together. In fact, we are always at our best when we cooperate with eagerness and joyful humility. This is especially true when it comes to helping our brothers and sisters in Christ who are struggling.

#2: ENCOURAGE REPLANTERS AND THEIR FAMILIES

Replanting is not for everyone. It takes a particular gift mix and a clear calling from the Lord. And, like every other ministry, serving as a pastor of a church replant can be at times very discouraging. There are ups and downs when replanting a congregation. It can be discouraging when young families come and visit but don't stay because you can't offer the same types of children's programming that the large church down the street does. It is discouraging when it seems like the congregation is not catching your vision for living on mission and reaching the lost in the community. It can be discouraging when it feels like even the smallest change you try to implement is met with pushback for all kinds of silly reasons.

While it is critical to intentionally encourage and care for replanters, it is just as important to care for and support the replanter's wife and children. Ministry of any kind can be very hard on a pastor's family. Replanting a church brings unique pressures and challenges that not only affect the replanter but affect his wife and kids as well. This is why it is so vital to have Christian brothers and sisters, like you, who intentionally encourage these replanters and their families over the long haul. Let's consider several practical ways you can do just this.

Write notes of encouragement.

Few things are more encouraging than a kind, uplifting word from a friend. This is why notes of encouragement are so powerful. Perhaps you can get others from your church involved in this ministry and periodically throughout the year send a large bundle of encouragement notes to the replanter and his family. Whatever it looks like, this is a simple but powerful way to care for this dear family.

Send gift cards and flowers.

Another way to regularly encourage a replanter's wife and kids is to surprise them with special gifts periodically. Gift cards to a favorite local restaurant, toy store, book store, gift store, or spa (for *mom,* of course) might be exactly what they need. Sending a bouquet of flowers from time to time is a simple, thoughtful gesture to express your care for the replanter's wife as well. Be intentional about surprising them with these types of thoughtful gifts.

Let them know when you pray for them.

One of the most powerful and encouraging things you can do for a replanter and his family is to pray for them intentionally and consistently. Regularly ask them how you can pray for them specifically. Be sure to let them know you are lifting them up to the Lord on a regular basis. Perhaps you can share specific prayer requests with others in your church who can join you in praying for this family.

Surprise them with a book or magazine.

Select a "book of the month" or subscribe to magazines and devotional guides to send to the replanter, his wife and children. This will be an ongoing source of encouragement and edification for them. This communicates intentional care for their spiritual growth in the Lord, especially in the midst of ministry challenges that are sure to come.

Invite the replanter's wife to women's events.

A powerful way to encourage the replanter's wife is to find a way for her to take part in special women's events that are happening in other churches. Special retreats or conferences that women in your church will be attending, for instance, are great events to invite her to join in on. The reality is this: chances are that in the replant there will be very few opportunities for her to focus on her own spiritual growth and fellowship with other godly women. You and your church can help immensely with this.

Text message reminders of God's promises.

God's Word is so encouraging. Make it a habit to remind the replanter and his family of the specific promises of God and other wonderful truths in Scripture. As followers of Jesus, we can be very forgetful. We need to be reminded regularly of who God is and who we are in Christ. As the Apostle Peter wrote to fellow believers in 2 Peter 1:12, *"I will always remind you of these things, even though you know them and are firmly established in the truth you now have."*

Give them a phone call once in awhile.

While notes of encouragement are powerful, spoken words of love and encouragement are even more so. There is nothing like hearing words from someone who cares about you that build you up. A phone call doesn't need to be super long, it just needs to happen! Even if you are not a big talker, I want to encourage you to be an agent of God's love and encouragement in the life of this family! Recruit others from your church who can join you in this. Trust me, these phone calls will be a source of great joy not only for the replanter and his family, but for you as well.

Send birthday cards.

Who doesn't love to get a birthday card? Sending personal birthday cards is a wonderful reminder to this family that they are loved and that others are thinking about them. Be sure to send a fun little gift with their birthday card as well!

A few more encouragement ideas...

To encourage the whole family:

- Zoo Day
- Professional Baseball Game Day
- Weekend in the Mountains or at the Beach
- Amusement Park/Water Park Day
- Surprise Cookie Tray/Popcorn/Cupcakes Sent to the Family
- Family Movie Night at Home Package – (Redbox, Pizza, Popcorn)

To encourage the replanter's wife:

- Starbucks Gift Card and a Book
- Gift Certificate to have the House Cleaned
- Spa Gift Card
- Surprise Lunch with other Pastor's/Leader's Wives

#3: SERVE A REPLANT AS A VOLUNTEER

One of the greatest ways you can get involved in helping a replant is by serving as a volunteer in some capacity. What a joy it will be for you to serve this congregation! Likewise, it will be a great blessing for the replanter and members of the replant to have you come and serve.

You will want to touch base with the replanting pastor and ask how you can best serve this replant. My guess is that there will be a large various of ways this replant can put you to work, particularly at their weekend worship gathering. They may need your help with anything from leading music, to holding babies in the nursery, to serving on the greeting team, to cleaning some classrooms, to running computer slides in the service, to helping with administrative tasks, to making a repair on the building. Whatever it might look like, replants are always in need of volunteer help. Your willingness to serve will be a great blessing to this congregation!

#4. JOIN THE CORE TEAM OF A NEW REPLANT

We were not made to minister in the church alone, and the Bible is clear on this. This is particularly true when it comes to replanting a congregation—a replanting pastor and his family cannot do this all on their own. It is not possible. They need help. This is why a core team is absolutely essential to the ongoing health, stability, and growth of any church replant.

What is a core team?

Simply put, a core team are those individuals who serve as the committed members and servants working together with the replanter to lead this new replant. It is made up of men and women, boys and girls who are all-in with this replant. While there will be folks whose excitement and commitment may wane, the core team are those individuals who have made a commitment to be part of this new church regardless of the challenges that lie ahead. This is why they are called the core team—they serve as the core of this replant.

Who makes up the core team?

Ideally, this core team will be made up of individuals from several groups of people: Existing members of the declining congregation, the replanting pastor and his family, and individuals from the community and other congregations who feel called to be part of this replant. This last group is made up folks just like you! The greater representation the core team has from these different groups of people, the better. It is healthy to have a team made up of those with diverse giftings, passions, and backgrounds. Older folks and younger folks, those who have been part of church their whole life, and those who are brand new to this whole Christian thing. Both those who are feeling tired and discouraged, and those who have fresh passionate vision for what lies ahead have an important role to play on the core team. With Christ at the center and a commitment toward love and unity amongst the core team, God will do amazing things through this group of committed servants.

What is the commitment for those on a core team?

While the commitment is going to be different depending on the particular replant, there are some basic commitments you can anticipate if you choose to be part of a core team. In my experience, the following foundational commitments are shared by those who make up the most effective core teams in church replanting.

First of all, each core team member commits to serving as a minister in various ways. This means working with the replanting pastor and the other members of the core team to find a place to serve the body of the replant. This new congregation will need people to serve in a wide variety of ministry areas. It might be serving as greeters, musicians, sound technicians, slide runners, children's ministry leaders or helpers, making coffee, leading a small group or adult Sunday School, etc. This replant needs people who are willing to step up to serve in ministry in a variety of different ways.

Secondly, each potential team member must understand they are expected to live and serve as missionaries to the community. Remember, the driving purpose for replanting this church is mission. To reach people who are far from God with the Gospel! This means those who feel called to be part of this replant core team will be expected to go show and tell the gospel boldly to their family, friends, and neighbors. This should not be a burden but a joy for those who make up this team!

Consider the joy of replanting.

While potential core team members must count the cost to being part of this team, they must also consider the excitement and great privilege that comes with being part of it as well. There are very few greater catalysts for joy than being used by God to make Jesus known in the lives of others. It's so thrilling to see people who are far from God come to know and treasure Jesus and then invite others to do the same. Core team members must lead the way in this.

Remember how God saved you? Remember the joy of knowing Jesus and his incredible love for you in those first days, months, perhaps years of your salvation? Someone from some church introduced you to Jesus and then you were discipled by that church. The person who introduced you to Jesus and the church that you connected to rejoiced when God saved you – the angels rejoiced, Jesus rejoiced, God the Father rejoiced, the Holy Spirit rejoiced! This is the amazing work God has called core teams to lead as they help launch a new replant. Ask the Lord if being part of a replant core team is what he is calling you to. Yes, there is great commitment involved, but there is even greater joy.

WHAT IS GOD CALLING YOU TO DO?

Each and every replant needs the ongoing support of believers just like you. What does this look like? How can you, and perhaps your church, get involved in the replanting of dying churches? Consider making a commitment to at least one of the following:

1. Pray for particular replants and their leaders.
2. Encourage replanters and their families.
3. Serve a replant as a volunteer.
4. Join the core team of a new replant.

May the Lord, by his grace and power, give you a burden to love, serve, pray for, and partner with a replant with the intentional, radical, selfless, love of Jesus over the long haul.

FOR FURTHER REFLECTION

1. Replanting can be discouraging, lonely & hard work - write down a few ways right now that you and your church can encourage, befriend, and ease the work of a replanting pastor and his family.

2. What are some of the strengths of your church that will make it easy to come alongside the replanted church to help? In what ways is your church going to have to sacrifice or step out in faith to come alongside to help the replanted church?

3. 3.As you read through the four different ways to get involved in replanting presented in this chapter, what gets you most excited? Where might you feel called to serve in this season of your life? Are there other ways you can imagine helping out with a replant?

Chapter 5

IS GOD CALLING ME TO REPLANT?

(considerations for potential replanting pastors)

In his book, *The Salvation of Souls*, Jonathan Edwards writes about the importance of honestly evaluating one's readiness for pastoral ministry. His words apply to every replanter,

> "Those that are about to undertake this work should do it with the greatest seriousness and consideration of the vast importance of the work, how great a thing it is to have the care of precious souls committed to them, and with a suitable concern upon their minds, considering the great difficulties, dangers, and temptations that do accompany it. It is compared to going to warfare."[1]

As with every pastoral position, it is critical that potential replanters honestly assess and evaluate whether or not they are called to this unique and challenging ministry. Perhaps you are a pastor or pastor in training and are wondering if God might be calling you to replant a dying church. What are the qualifications? What gifts are needed? Is there a particular wiring that is best suited for replanting?

Along with the clear, biblical qualifications for a pastor as laid out in the Pastoral Epistles, there are at least eight additional characteristics that must be present in those seeking to lead and shepherd a replant. These characteristics are key indicators of whether an individual is prepared, equipped and ready to effectively lead healthy revitalization in a replanting context.[2] Let's consider each of these.

CHARACTERISTIC #1: VISIONARY SHEPHERD

What is a visionary shepherd? A visionary shepherd has the ability to sense and see God's next steps for a congregation and the capacity to lead the church forward as a loving shepherd. He is patient, wise, strategic, and relational. What we see in a visionary shepherd is not someone who can simply dream big dreams, start new things, and get people pumped along the way. If a replanter is all visionary without a passion to shepherd souls, he will fail to win the hearts and the trust of the people. He will likely cause a big mess in his replanting efforts. He may have great ideas but is unwilling to do the hard work of doing the things needed to make those ideas become reality. Or worse, he may be unwilling to do the things he is asking others to do. The result of this kind of leadership over time is a lack of respect and trust on the part of the congregation toward this replanter. Sadly, all too often, this kind of behavior will get him fired or end up splitting the church. Being a visionary is important, but it's not enough by itself in replanting.

At the same time, it's not enough to only be a shepherd. A shepherd is someone who loves and cares for the flock. In many ways a good shepherd has the characteristics of a good chaplain - pastoral, caring, and gentle. This is an important role of a replanter. However, just as many chaplains are trained and gifted to help people process in a severe moment of crisis and spiritual need, replanters who are almost all shepherd without any real visionary leadership gifting, often end up helping congregations die due to a lack of vision rather than leading them back to life.

While each replanter is unique and will lean more toward either visionary or shepherd in their natural gifting, the most effective replanters are not exclusively one or the other. Rather, they are a combination of both: Visionary-shepherds. This is unique wiring, I realize. This is someone who is excited about the future, who can cast a vision, and can lead people toward that vision in a compelling and winsome manner. At the same time, they must love people well, shepherding folks along the way toward this vision with patience, humility, discernment, and great care.

CHARACTERISTIC #2: CAPACITY FOR SUFFERING

The ups and downs of replanting take a toll on the replanter spiritually, physically, emotionally, relationally, and financially. The pain of replanting necessitates an ability to persevere and endure the high cost of ministry as God uses the replanter to turn a dying church around.

We just need to be honest about the fact that if a man feels called to pursue replanting and go into a church revitalization context, it must be understood from the beginning that this will not be an easy calling. This is a hard calling, which is why it is so vital for a replanter and his family to humbly and honestly count the cost before jumping in. As you consider replanting, you must be mindful of the need for a maturity that understands suffering is going to be part of this call. An ability to wisely evaluate the potential challenges that lie ahead not only for yourself personally, but for the congregation and for your family.

Yet in the midst of the challenges and suffering that can come in church replanting, there is also great joy! As we read in James 1, "Consider it pure joy when you face trials of many kinds because the testing of your faith develops perseverance." There is a very real sense in which we are called to enter into Christ's sufferings with joy for the sake of his people and the Gospel, just as Christ has suffered for us.

As with any vocational calling within the church or para-church – whether it's youth ministry, children's ministry, worship ministry, small group ministry, or church replanting – we need to understand that suffering is part of this calling. Because of this, potential replanters enter into the vocation of church replanting wisely, thoughtfully, and prayerfully. Developing a solid, Biblical theology of suffering is vital in helping replanters persevere through the dark times that are sure to come.

CHARACTERISTIC #3: AFFINITY FOR LEGACY/HISTORY

Most dying churches have bright spots in their history, seasons of health and growth that older members still look back on with great delight. Perhaps it was a time when this church was having a Gospel-centered impact on children or youth or the poor in their communities. These are precious memories for remaining folks in this congregation. It is critical that a replanter not only understands and acknowledges the history and legacy of the church they want to replant, but they must also value and even enjoy that church's history. He must seek to remind the church of it and to honor it when and where possible, and then build upon the legacy of those who were there before him.

One of the ways a replanter can get into hot water quickly is by ignoring the church's history or giving the congregation the impression that he doesn't appreciate the past. This mistake is very common and can happen in a number of different ways. As one example, it is common for some replanters to give the impression that they really dislike the building. They're always talking about how old it is and how they need to change the building in this way or that way to make it more relevant and inviting. I don't doubt that most replanters have some legitimate concerns about their building needing to be updated, but they must be careful in how they communicate this with the folks who have been there for years. Remember, these are the men and women who have often sacrificed to build and paint walls in this building, replaced the windows, put in new carpet, washed the pew cushions, and sacrificially given of their finances to help pay the mortgage for the purpose of Gospel ministry. They love this building—it is part of their history. Most likely, many of these folks realize that some changes need to be made to the building, however, they need to be led to help make these changes by a pastor who is careful, patient and appreciates their dedication to this building.

The most effective replanters are celebrators of a church's history. They desire to build off this history, not erase it. Where a replanter is going to get people excited and give hope to a dying church isn't simply by looking ahead to what could be. It's also in looking at what has already been—what God has already done in this congregation. It's celebrating the future and the past; dreaming and remembering together. This is why a replanter must love letting folks share stories and celebrate the wonderful things God has done through their church in the past, especially with older members. To share the story once again about that Easter back in 1968 when the neighborhood drunk finally gave church a chance, Jesus saved him, and he was baptized the next week. I mean, these are the types of stories that need to be remembered and celebrated. These are the stories that help renew hope and vision for the future. Helping people see that God's not dead and not done with their church. He's alive! God was alive back then, he's alive now, and he'll be alive in the future! This is what it looks like for a replanter to love and build off of a church's past without allowing people in the congregation to idolize it in an unhealthy way.

CHARACTERISTIC #4: MULTI-GENERATIONAL CAPACITY

In replanting, it is important that the replanter is comfortable ministering to folks of all different ages. He must be able to connect fairly easily with both the young and old in his congregation so each group knows they are loved, valued and heard, and so all ages are pastored well. Again, this is a difference that is often seen between most church plants and replants—often times in a new church plant, the congregation looks a lot like the pastor and his family in terms of age, stage of life, etc. In a replanting context, however, ministry typically happens with multi-generational congregants, which is an amazing opportunity even in the face of real challenges. I truly believe the church is at its best when it's multi-generational. In replanting, there are unique challenges that accompany this type of multi-generational reality, and yet at the same time, unique joys.

Practically then, the replanter must be someone who can hang out with and encourage the nine-year-old and the ninety-year-old. Someone who feels comfortable going to the hospital when someone is dying and also showing up to watch a 3rd grader play her first soccer game. They must be an individual who is gifted and eager to float in either of these types of contexts among many others. This doesn't mean that the replanter must be off the charts gifted in ministering to every age group—it's humbly recognizing the fact that he has been called to be a pastor for the whole church. To love those of all ages and to be involved in the lives of the sheep under his care.

CHARACTERISTIC #5: RESOURCEFUL GENERALIST

What does it mean to be a resourceful generalist? Scant resources, limited budgets, small or non-existent staff and absent or out of date technology are standard features in a dying and declining church. That's not a shock, right? Replanters wear many hats. They know how to get things done, gather resources and do the best with what they have in front of them. The lack of available resources should not reduce their efforts, energy, or impact to love and lead their people well.

A replanter is going into a situation where resources are limited on all kinds of levels. This means the replanter must be a generalist, willing to do whatever it takes to shepherd this church. The replanter must recognize, "Hey, I may be the custodian, secretary, preacher, worship leader, and the middle school Sunday School teacher all on the same Sunday! This is part of the calling to replant!" The replanter must be willing to say, "Whatever you need, God. Whatever this church needs, I'm willing to do." That's really what I'm getting at when describing a resourceful generalist: A humble, servant's heart that is willing to do whatever is needed and whatever it takes to lovingly lead this church back to health.

This might mean serving in areas that are not your favorite places to serve and doing things you'd rather not do. It means leading areas of ministry outside of your comfort zone. A resourceful generalist does the best they can with what they have. But at the same time, this doesn't mean they seek to do everything themselves. It means equipping others in the gifting God has given them and unleashing them to serve in various ways as well. A resourceful generalist is a servant leader willing to model sacrificial, joyful service before anyone else in the congregation. No task is beneath them. The congregation knows and sees this in the way the replanter leads this church.

CHARACTERISTIC #6: TACTICAL PATIENCE

Progress and pace are different in church replanting. Some things can be addressed immediately; others have to wait—either for the congregation to be ready to move or for the resources to be present. A replanter is continually looking toward what is up ahead and is seeking to help the congregation move forward, yet they know that timing and patience are key in bringing the church along. Tactical patience understands that waiting is not wasted time.

There are two key components to this idea of tactical patience. One is timing, the other is patient wisdom. It's not one or the other that's needed to lead a replant, but both. Tactical patience comes in knowing the timing of when to change something in the church, and also when not to change something. Knowing when to say something, and when not to say something. What hills are hills to die on, and which aren't.

At the heart of tactical patience is wisdom and discernment that is ours only through the power and leading of the Holy Spirit. Tactical patience means knowing the right and a wrong time to make a decision or to have a conversation, being patient enough to wait on God's timing to address that issue.

CHARACTERISTIC #7: EMOTIONAL INTELLIGENCE

Replanting a church, as with ministry in general, is all about people. It involves a lot of understanding, relating to, and caring for all different types of people created in the image of God. Ministry is people-work. The reason why many pastors fail in the church is not because they don't know enough Bible and theology, it's because they aren't good with people. They may be overly awkward with people or not realize that many perceive him as being mad all the time because he seems to always carry a scowl on his face. The sad part is, they are probably not even aware of it! It's a lack of emotional intelligence.

There is no better indicator for success in relationships within our ministries than one's emotional intelligence. But what exactly is emotional intelligence? Emotional intelligence, defined by the Oxford Dictionary, is the capacity to be aware of, control, and express one's emotions, and to handle interpersonal relationships judiciously and empathetically. At its core, emotional intelligence consists of the following four leadership skills or competencies:

1. *Self-Awareness:* The ability to know yourself and your emotions, not as you wish they were, but as they *really* are.

2. *Self-Regulation:* The wisdom and ability to understand the impact you have when you take action or refrain from action.

3. *Social Awareness:* The ability to read other people and understand their emotions.

4. *Relationship Management:* The ability to incorporate the other three skills to navigate and build positive relationships with all types of people, in one-on-one and group settings.

At the heart of emotional intelligence are lifelong skills that allow a replanting pastor to be more empathetic and have better interpersonal relationships. Personal growth in emotional intelligence helps replanters love people well, speak in an appropriate tone that brings comfort or correction, and to practice being more patient and caring with those in our ministry that are difficult to love and lead. These are skills absolutely vital in replanting a dying congregation. Emotional intelligence is a must for a replanter to be effective in leading healthy change.

CHARACTERISTIC #8: SPOUSAL SUPPORT

A replanter isn't alone in his calling. He understands that his spouse will serve an important role in supporting him as well as the family while he is leading the church. The replanter's wife possesses a love for Jesus and the church and is committed for the long haul, understanding the road of ministry will be full of ups and downs. Perhaps most importantly, the replanter's spouse must be emotionally and spiritually prepared for the challenges that come with replanting a dying church.

Exercise: Marriage and Ministry Self-Assessment

The following is a self-assessment to help you as someone considering replanting, along with your wife, honestly reflect on your potential calling to this vital ministry. These ten questions are valuable for each of you to answer, evaluating your responses together as individuals and as a couple. While several of these questions are directly targeted to you as the potential replanter, it is helpful for your wife to share insight and input from her perspective as your wife and best friend. It is recommended to have one or two other couples from your church sit down with the two of you to discuss your responses to these questions.

10 Questions to Ask Before Pursuing a Church Replant

1. *Do I see this opportunity as a mission field?*

2. *Am I emotionally mature enough to take upon myself the rigors of taking the lead role in a church?*

3. *Am I biblically and theologically competent enough to lead this congregation?*

4. *Am I organizationally competent?*

5. *How will I respond to and love my critics?*

6. *Will I make a commitment for the long haul, through good and bad?*

7. *Will I be a continuous learner about church revitalization and pastoral leadership?*

8. *Am I committed to being a positive example and encourager for my family on this journey?*

9. *Do I have pastoral mentors who can coach and encourage me?*

10. *Do I have a sufficient support system of peer relationships and friends?*

FOR FURTHER REFLECTION

1. Take a minute to reflect on your life & share about a pastor who had a major impact on you - what were 2 of the qualities that made him a great pastor?

2. How do you think he gained those two qualities in his personality & ministry?

3. What are your thoughts and feelings about the Jonathan Edwards quote that compares going into ministry to going into warfare? Agree or disagree? Why?

4. As you look at the 8 characteristics of a replanter, how would you assess yourself? Where are strong? Where do you need to grow? Any that stand out to you that you may not have thought of before?

NOTES

CHAPTER 1 — WHAT IS CHURCH REPLANTING?

[1] Toni Ridgaway, "Statistics Don't Tell the Whole Story When It Comes to Church Attendance," *ChurchLeaders.com*, accessed September 12, 2015, http://www.churchleaders.com/pastors/pastor-articles/170739-statistics-don-t-tell-the-whole-story-when-it-comes-to-church-attendance.html.

[2] Ibid.

[3] Dan Bensen, "You Lost Me," *TheGospelCoalition.org*, accessed May 3, 2017, https://www.thegospelcoalition.org/article/you_lost_me.

[4] Thom Rainer, "13 Issues for 2013," *ChurchLeaders.com*, accessed June 15, 2016, http://churchleaders.com/pastors/pastor-articles/164787-thom-rainer-13-issues-churches-2013.html.

[5] Meredith Yackel, "Replant Lab Aims at Reducing Number of Dying Churches," *BPNews.net*, accessed May 3, 2017, http://www.bpnews.net/47483/replant-lab-aims-at-reducing-number-of-dying-churches.

[6] Ibid.

[7] _____ , "Church Replanting," *Namb.net*, accessed May 3, 2017, https://www.namb.net/church-replanting.

[8] Ibid.

[9] Al Moher, "A Guide to Church Revitalization," *SBTS.edu*, accessed January 7, 2017, http://www.sbts.edu/press/a-guide-to-church-revitalization/#download.

CHAPTER 2 — WHY IS REPLANTING SO IMPORTANT?

[1] Matt Schmucker, "Why Revitalize?," *9marks.org*, accessed August 5, 2016. https://9marks.org/article/journalwhy-revitalize/.

[2] Ibid.

[3] Mark Clifton, "Dying Churches Matter to God… and to NAMB," *Namb.net*, accessed September 1, 2016, https://www.namb.net/send-network-blog/dying-churches-matter-to-god-and-to-namb.

CHAPTER 3 — WHAT DOES GOD SAY ABOUT REPLANTING CHURCHES?

[1] Charles Spurgeon, "Made Perfect in Weakness," *Truthforlife.org*, accessed November 4, 2016, https://www.truthforlife.org/resources/daily-devotionals/11/4/1881/.

[2] Ibid.

[3] Ibid.

[4] Bill Henard, *Can These Bones Live?* (Nashville, TN: B&H Publishing Group, 2015), 2.

[5] Ibid.

[6] Mark Clifton, "Dying Churches Matter to God... and to NAMB", *Namb.net*, accessed September 1, 2016, https://www.namb.net/send-network-blog/dying-churches-matter-to-god-and-to-namb.

[7] See Rick Warren, "The Five Stages of Renewal in the Local Church," *Pastors.com*, accessed January 24, 2018, http://pastors.com/the-five-stages-of-renewal-in-the-local-church/.

[8] Ibid.

CHAPTER 5 — IS GOD CALLING ME TO REPLANT?

[1] Jonathan Edwards, *The Salvation of Souls* (Wheaton, IL: Crossway, 2002), 51-52.

[2] These eight characteristics were identified and defined by the National NAMB Replant team in 2015.

Get the resource which is empowering a movement of church revitalization.

"Mark Hallock is one of the most important voices in this unprecedented need in the modern day to revitalize dying churches. *Replant Roadmap* is sure to become the practical how-to guide to lead this next generation into this noble work."

Brian Croft, Senior Pastor, Auburndale Baptist Church; Senior Fellow, Church Revitalization Center, The Southern Baptist Theological Seminary

the Replant Series

This series features short, action-oriented resources aimed at equipping the North American church for a movement of church replanting, introduced by Pastor Mark Hallock's book *Replant Roadmap*.

Thousands of churches are closing their doors in United States every year in some of its fastest-growing, most under-reached neighborhoods. Yet there is much hope for these churches, particularly through the biblically-rooted, gospel-saturated work of replanting.

Designed for both group and individual study, these books will help you understand what the Bible has to say about how God builds and strengthens his church and offer you some practical steps toward revitalization in your own.

For more information, visit **acomapress.org** and **nonignorable.org**

ACOMA PRESS

Acoma Press exists to make Jesus non-ignorable by equipping and encouraging churches through gospel-centered resources.

Toward this end, each purchase of an Acoma Press resource serves to catalyze disciple-making and to equip leaders in God's Church. In fact, a portion of your purchase goes directly to funding planting and replanting efforts in North America and beyond. To see more of our current resources, visit us at *acomapress.org*.

Thank you.

Made in the USA
Columbia, SC
27 February 2018